George Washington's Prayers

Robert W. Pelton

$9.95

Cover Design: Kathleen Widdowson

kafleenvs@aol.com

Freedom & Liberty Foundation Press

First Edition

3

Proudly Printed in America
On Recycled Paper
In
Charleston, South Carolina

Proudly Published in America
By
Freedom & Liberty Foundation
Press
In
Knoxville. Tennessee

About the Author

Robert W. Pelton has been writing and lecturing for more than 45 years on historical, humor *religious* and other subjects.

He's published numerous articles and more than 150 books..

Pelton has carefully mined hundreds of sources for historical cooking and baking recipes from the early days of America.

He's perused innumerable old cookbooks as well as yellowed and tattered handwritten receipt ledgers from both private and public archives and libraries.

Through all this, he's been able to skillfully recreate these recipe treasures of the past in 14 historical cook books.

For a Power Point Presentation covering the *Words, Dreams, Beliefs, and Aspirations of Our Founding Fathers* or *Cooking and Baking in the American Colonies* contact Mr. Pelton at 910-339-5354; or 865-776-6644; or by email: *christianamerica2@yahoo.com*

Contents

1. Introducing George
            Washington's Prayers   11
Washington's Character
                As a Youngster   21

3. What Washington Wrote & Spoke   41

4. Other Quotes of Great Interest   55

5. Prayers of Washington While a
            General and as President   63

Other Titles by This Author   85

1

Introducing George Washington's Prayers

I want to make special note of Washington's spiritual life.

He dutifully recorded the words of advice his mother, Mary, gave him when he was leaving home to begin what would turn out to be a lifelong service to his country.

She instructed her son with these words: *"Remember that God is our only one trust.*

"To Him, I commend you ...

"My son, neglect not the duty of secret prayer."

Did George Washington heed his mother's admonition?

Of course he did!

Here's what he in turn said about her: *"My mother was the most beautiful woman I ever saw.*

"All I am I owe to my mother.

"I attribute all my success in life to the moral, intellectual and physical education I received from her."

Throughout his life, whether while a young man, Commander-in-Chief of the Continental Army, or President of the United States, George Washington showed, by example, how meaningful were his mother's teachings.

He'd stand up at promptly 9:00 pm, take his candle, and go off by himself.

There, from 9:00pm to 10:00pm, he wouldn't be seen.

He was alone on his knees in front of a chair praying.

A candle stood on a stand next to the chair.

And his *Bible* was open before him.

This he'd do even when guests were present.

Then promptly at 10:00pm, he'd emerge and go directly to his bedroom.

He'd get up every morning at 4:00am, and spend another hour in the same room.

William White commented on the personal life of Washington's in his book, *Washington's Writing:* *"It seems proper to subjoin to this letter what was told to me by Mr. Robert Lewis, at Fredericksburg, in the year 1827.*

"Being a nephew of Washington and his private secretary during the first part of his presidency, Mr. Lewis lived with him on terms of intimacy, and had the best opportunity for observing his habits.

"Mr. Lewis said that he'd accidentally witnessed his private devotions in his library both morning and evening; that on those occasions he'd seen him in a kneeling posture with a Bible open before him, and that he believed such to have been his daily practice."

Washington made a practice of *never* traveling unnecessarily on the Sabbath.

He *never*, no matter what the circumstances, received visitors on Sunday, with one exception, a Godly friend named Trumbel.

They'd spend time reading the *Bible* and praying together.

Henry Muhlenberg was the pastor of the Lutheran church near Valley Forge.

He was also one of the founders of the Lutheran Church in America.

He said this about Washington while he was in command of the Continental Army: *"I heard a fine example today, namely, that His Excellency General Washington rode around among his army yesterday and admonished each and every one to fear God, to put away the wickedness that has set in and become so general, and to practice the Christian virtues.*

"From all appearances, this gentleman does not belong to the so-called world of society, for he respects God's Word, believes in the atonement through Christ, and bears himself in humility and gentleness.

"Therefore, the Lord God has also singularly, yea, marvelously, preserved him from harm in the midst of countless perils, ambuscades, fatigues, etc.,

16

and has hitherto graciously held him in His hand as a chosen vessel."

Washington, *"without making ostentatious professions of religion, was a sincere believer in the Christian faith, and a truly devout man,"* according to John Marshall, first Chief Justice of the United States Supreme Court.

Marshall had fought with General Washington at Valley Forge during the War for Independence.

After Washington died on December 4, 1799, Reverend J. T. Kirkland said: *"The virtues of our departed friend were crowned by piety.*

"He is known to have been habitually devout.

"To Christian institutions he gave the countenance of his, example; and no one could express, more fully, his sense of the Providence of God, and the dependence of man."

Praying at Valley Forge

The paintings of George Washington kneeling in prayer in the snow covered woods of Valley Forge are based on fact. We have all probably heard of his prayer that was overheard by a Quaker, a pacifist, a Tory – a man loyal to the Crown. This man returned home shaken and said to his wife: *"Our cause is lost! I came unexpectedly in the woods upon a man who was kneeling in prayer. As I drew closer, I heard his voice. I heard the impassioned plea of his prayers and saw the tears on his cheeks. I knew our cause was lost."*

The Quaker and his wife were so overwhelmed that they became supporters of Washington and the American cause.

A slightly different version of this same story comes from William J. Fedder's *America's God and Country:*

"In 1777 while the American army lay at Valley Forge, a good old Quaker by the name of Potts had occasion to pass through a thick woods near headquarters.

"As he traversed the dark brown forest, he heard, at a distance before him, a voice which as he advanced became more fervid.

"Approaching with slowness and

circumspection, whom should he behold in a dark bower, apparently formed for the purpose, but the Commander-in-Chief of the armies of the United Colonies on his knees in the act of devotion to the Ruler of the Universe!

"At the moment when Friend Potts, concealed by the trees, came up, Washington was interceding for his beloved country.

"With tones of gratitude that labored for adequate expression he adored that exuberant goodness which, from the depth of obscurity, had exalted him to the head of a great nation, and that nation fighting at fearful odds for all the world holds dear.

"Soon as the General had finished his devotions and had retired, Friend Potts returned to his house, and threw himself into a chair by the side of his wife. "'Heigh! Isaac!' said she with tenderness, *'thee seems agitated; what's the matter?'*

"'Indeed, my dear' quoth he, *'if I appear agitated 'tis no more than what I have seen this day what I shall never forget.*

"Till now I have bought that a Christian and a soldier were characters incompatible; but if George Washington be not a man of God, l am mistaken, and still more shall I be disappointed if God does not through him perform some great thing for this country.'"

Washington's Oath and Actions

When Washington took his oath of office as President of the United States, he subsequently bent  forward and kissed the *Bible* on which he had just taken his oath.

The *Bible* was opened to the *Book of Genesis.*

He then led the Senate and the House of Representatives to the church for a two hour worship service.

References to God

Used more than 80 different names in reference to God in his prayers and his writings. They included:

All Wise Dispenser of Events

Beneficent Author of the Universe

The God of Armies

Author of All Good

Eternal Lord God

Most Gracious God

Thy Divine Majesty

King of Heaven

"So Help Me God," following the required oath of office was initiated by Washington.

2

Washington's Character As a Youngster

George Washington was school boy age in Virginia when he set out to meticulously copy a list of 110 rules.

He titled his list *"Rules of Civility & Decent Behavior in Company and Conversation."*

These rules were based on a set of rules compiled by Jesuit teachers in the 16th-century.

This is the point in his life where Washington initially showed an inclination of future greatness.

According to historian Richard Brookhiser, these 110 rules were *"one of the earliest and most powerful forces to shape America's first president."*

Most of the rules concisely cover proper etiquette.

They offer suggestions on how one should act when eating in public and how to address one's superiors.

These rules also cover how to walk, how to dress, how to address one's superiors.

And they also address moral issues.

Brookhiser believes these rules are still applicable today just as they were in the past.

This man says the advice the rules offer, though often outlandish in detail, is still applicable in our day and age: *"Maybe they can work on us in our century as the Jesuits intended them to work in theirs."*

Rules of Civility & Decent Behavior
In Company and Conversation

Note: *Spelling and punctuation have been pdated for ease of reading.*

1. Every action done in company ought to be with some sign of respect to those that are present.

2. When in company, put not your hands to any part of the body not usually discovered.

3. Show nothing to your friend that may affright him.

4. In the presence of others, sing not to yourself with a humming voice, or drum with your fingers or feet.

5. If you cough, sneeze, sigh or yawn, do it not loud but privately, and speak not in your yawning, but put your handkerchief or hand before your face and turn aside.

6. Sleep not when others speak, sit not when others stand, speak not when you should hold your peace, walk not on when others stop.

7. Put not off your clothes in the presence of others, nor go out of your chamber half dressed.

8. At play and attire, it's good manners to give place to the last comer, and affect not to speak louder than ordinary.

9. Spit not into the fire, nor stoop low before it; neither put your hands into the flames to warm them, nor set your feet upon the fire, especially if there be meat before it.

10. When you sit down, keep your feet firm and even, without putting one on the other or crossing them.

11. Shift not yourself in the sight of others, nor gnaw your nails.

12. Shake not the head, feet, or legs; roll not the eyes; lift not one eyebrow higher than the other, wry not the mouth, and bedew no man's face with your spittle by approaching too near him when you speak.

13. Kill no vermin, or fleas, lice, ticks, etc. in the sight of others; if you see any filth or thick spittle put your foot dexterously upon it; if it be upon the clothes of your companions, put it off privately, and if it be upon your own clothes, return thanks to him who puts it off.

14. Turn not your back to others, especially in speaking; jog not the table or desk on which another reads or writes; lean not upon anyone.

15. Keep your nails clean and short, also your hands and teeth clean, yet without showing any great concern for them.

16. Do not puff up the cheeks, loll not out the tongue with the hands or beard, thrust out the lips or bite them, or keep the lips too open or too close.

17. Be no flatterer, neither play with any that delight not to be played withal.

18. Read no letter, books, or papers in company, but when there is a necessity for the doing of it, you must ask leave; come not near the books or writings of another so as to read them unless desired, or give your opinion of them unasked. Also look not nigh when another is writing a letter.

19. Let your countenance be pleasant but in serious matters somewhat grave.

20. The gestures of the body must be suited to the discourse you are upon.

21. Reproach none for the infirmities of nature, nor delight to put them that have in mind of thereof.

22. Show not yourself glad at the misfortune of another though he were your enemy.

23. When you see a crime punished, you may be inwardly pleased; but always show pity to the suffering offender.

24. Do not laugh too loud or too much at any public spectacle.

25. Superfluous compliments and all affectation of ceremonies are to be avoided, yet where due they are not to be neglected.

26. In putting off your hat to persons of distinction, as noblemen, justices, churchmen, etc., make a reverence, bowing more or less according to the custom of the better bred, and quality of the persons. Among your equals expect not always that they should begin with you first, but to pull off the hat when there is no need is affectation. In the manner of saluting and resaluting in words, keep to the most usual custom.

27. 'Tis ill manners to bid one more eminent than yourself be covered, as well as not to do it to whom it is due. Likewise he that makes too much haste to put on his hat does not well, yet he ought to put it on at the first, or at most the second time of being asked. Now what is herein spoken, of qualification in behavior in saluting, ought also to be observed in taking of

place and sitting down, for ceremonies without bounds are troublesome.

28. If anyone come to speak to you while you are are sitting stand up, though he be your inferior, and when you present seats, let it be to everyone according to his degree.

29. When you meet with one of greater quality than yourself, stop and retire, especially if it be at a door or any straight place, to give way for him to pass.

30. In walking, the highest place in most countries seems to be on the right hand; therefore, place yourself on the left of him whom you desire to honor. But if three walk together the middest place is the most honorable; the wall is usually given to the most worthy if two walk together.

31. If anyone far surpasses others, either in age, estate, or merit, yet would give place to a meaner than himself in his own lodging or elsewhere, the one ought not to except it. So he on the other part should not use much earnestness nor offer it above once or twice.

32. To one that is your equal, or not much inferior, you are to give the chief place in your lodging, and he to whom it is offered ought at the first to refuse it, but at the second to accept

though not without acknowledging his own unworthiness.

33. They that are in dignity or in office have in all places precedency, but whilst they are young, they ought to respect those that are their equals in birth or other qualities, though they have no public charge.

34. It is good manners to prefer them to whom we speak before ourselves, especially if they be above us, with whom in no sort we ought to begin.

35. Let your discourse with men of business be short and comprehensive.

36. Artificers and persons of low degree ought not to use many ceremonies to lords or others of high degree, but respect and highly honor then, and those of high degree ought to treat them with affability and courtesy, without arrogance.

37. In speaking to men of quality do not lean nor look them full in the face, nor approach too near them at left. Keep a full pace from them.

38. In visiting the sick, do not presently play the physician if you be not knowing therein.

39. In writing or speaking, give to every person his due title according to his degree and the custom of the place.

40. Strive not with your superior in argument, but always submit your judgment to others with modesty.

41. Undertake not to teach your equal in the art himself professes; it savors of arrogancy.

42. Let your ceremonies in courtesy be proper to the dignity of his place with whom you converse, for it is absurd to act the same with a clown and a prince.

43. Do not express joy before one sick in pain, for that contrary passion will aggravate his misery.

44. When a man does all he can, though it succeed not well, blame not him that did it.

45. Being to advise or reprehend any one, consider whether it ought to be in public or in private, and presently or at some other time; in what terms to do it; and in reproving show no signs of cholor but do it with all sweetness and mildness.

46. Take all admonitions thankfully in what time or place soever given, but afterwards not

being culpable take a time and place convenient to let him know it that gave them.

47. Mock not nor jest at any thing of importance. Break no jests that are sharp, biting, and if you deliver any thing witty and pleasant, abstain from laughing thereat yourself.

48. Wherein you reprove another be unblameable yourself, for example is more prevalent than precepts.

49. Use no reproachful language against any one; neither curse nor revile.

50. Be not hasty to believe flying reports to the disparagement of any.

51. Wear not your clothes foul, or ripped, or dusty, but see they be brushed once every day at least and take heed that you approach not to any uncleaness.

52. In your apparel be modest and endeavor to accommodate nature, rather than to procure admiration; keep to the fashion of your equals, such as are civil and orderly with respect to time and places.

53. Run not in the streets, neither go too slowly, nor with mouth open; go not shaking of arms, nor upon the toes, kick not the earth with

your feet, go not upon the toes, nor in a dancing fashion.

54. Play not the peacock, looking everywhere about you, to see if you be well decked, if your shoes fit well, if your stockings sit neatly and clothes handsomely.

55. Eat not in the streets, nor in the house, out of season.

56. Associate yourself with men of good quality if you esteem your own reputation; for 'tis better to be alone than in bad company.

57. In walking up and down in a house, only with one in company if he be greater than yourself, at the first give him the right hand and stop not till he does and be not the first that turns, and when you do turn let it be with your face towards him; if he be a man of great quality walk not with him cheek by jowl but somewhat behind him, but yet in such a manner that he may easily speak to you.

58. Let your conversation be without malice or envy, for 'tis a sign of a tractable and commendable nature, and in all causes of passion permit reason to govern.

59. Never express anything unbecoming, nor act against the rules moral before your inferiors.

60. Be not immodest in urging your friends to discover a secret.

61. Utter not base and frivolous things among grave and learned men, nor very difficult questions or subjects among the ignorant, or things hard to be believed; stuff not your discourse with sentences among your betters nor equals.

62. Speak not of doleful things in a time of mirth or at the table; speak not of melancholy things as death and wounds, and if others mention them, change if you can the discourse. Tell not your dreams, but to your intimate friend.

63. A man ought not to value himself of his achievements or rare qualities of wit; much less of his riches, virtue or kindred.

64. Break not a jest where none take pleasure in mirth; laugh not aloud, nor at all without occasion; deride no man's misfortune though there seem to be some cause.

65. Speak not injurious words neither in jest nor earnest; scoff at none although they give occasion.

66. Be not forward but friendly and courteous, the first to salute, hear and answer; and be not pensive when it's a time to converse.

67. Detract not from others, neither be excessive in commanding.

68. Go not thither, where you know not whether you shall be welcome or not; give not advice without being asked, and when desired do it briefly.

69. If two contend together take not the part of either unconstrained, and be not obstinate in your own opinion. In things indifferent be of the major side.

70. Reprehend not the imperfections of others, for that belongs to parents, masters and superiors.

71. Gaze not on the marks or blemishes of others and ask not how they came. What you may speak in secret to your friend, deliver not before others.

72. Speak not in an unknown tongue in company but in your own language and that as those of quality do and not as the vulgar. Sublime matters treat seriously.

73. Think before you speak, pronounce not imperfectly, nor bring out your words too hastily, but orderly and distinctly.

74. When another speaks, be attentive yourself and disturb not the audience. If any

hesitate in his words, help him not nor prompt him without desired. Interrupt him not, nor answer him till his speech be ended.

75. In the midst of discourse ask not of what one treats, but if you perceive any stop because of your coming, you may well entreat him gently to proceed. If a person of quality comes in while you're conversing, it's handsome to repeat what was said before.

76. While you are talking, point not with your finger at him of whom you discourse, nor approach too near him to whom you talk, especially to his face.

77. Treat with men at fit times about business and whisper not in the company of others.

78. Make no comparisons and if any of the company be commended for any brave act of virtue, commend not another for the same.

79. Be not apt to relate news if you know not the truth thereof. In discoursing of things you have heard, name not your author. Always a secret discover not.

80. Be not tedious in discourse or in reading unless you find the company pleased therewith.

81. Be not curious to know the affairs of others, neither approach those that speak in private.

82. Undertake not what you cannot perform but be careful to keep your promise.

83. When you deliver a matter do it without passion and with discretion, however mean the person be you do it to.

84. When your superiors talk to anybody hearken not, neither speak nor laugh.

85. In company of those of higher quality than yourself, speak not 'til you are asked a question, then stand upright, put off your hat and answer in few words.

86. In disputes, be not so desirous to overcome as not to give liberty to each one to deliver his opinion and submit to the judgment of the major part, especially if they are judges of the dispute.

87. Let your carriage be such as becomes a man grave, settled and attentive to that which is spoken. Contradict not at every turn what others say.

88. Be not tedious in discourse, make not many digressions, nor repeat often the same manner of discourse.

89. Speak not evil of the absent, for it is unjust.

90. Being set at meat scratch not, neither spit, cough or blow your nose except there's a necessity for it.

91. Make no show of taking great delight in your victuals. Feed not with greediness. Eat your bread with a knife. Lean not on the table, neither find fault with what you eat.

92. Take no salt or cut bread with your knife greasy.

93. Entertaining anyone at table it is decent to present him with meat. Undertake not to help others undesired by the master.

94. If you soak bread in the sauce, let it be no more than what you put in your mouth at a time, and blow not your broth at table but stay 'til it cools of itself.

95. Put not your meat to your mouth with your knife in your hand; neither spit forth the stones of any fruit pie upon a dish nor cast anything under the table.

96. It's unbecoming to heap much to one's mea. Keep your fingers clean and when foul wipe them on a corner of your table napkin.

97. Put not another bite into your mouth 'til the former be swallowed. Let not your morsels be too big for the jowls.

98. Drink not nor talk with your mouth full; neither gaze about you while you are drinking.

99. Drink not too leisurely nor yet too hastily. Before and after drinking wipe your lips. Breathe not then or ever with too great a noise, for it is uncivil.

100. Cleanse not your teeth with the tablecloth, napkin, fork or knife, but if others do it, let it be done with a pick tooth.

101. Rinse not your mouth in the presence of others.

102. It is out of use to call upon the company often to eat. Nor need you drink to others every time you drink.

103. In company of your betters be not longer in eating than they are. Lay not your arm but only your hand upon the table.

104. It belongs to the chiefest in company to unfold his napkin and fall to meat first. But he ought then to begin in time and to dispatch with dexterity that the slowest may have time allowed him.

105. Be not angry at table whatever happens and if you have reason to be so, show it not but on a cheerful countenance especially if there be strangers, for good humor makes one dish of meat a feast.

106. Set not yourself at the upper of the table but if it be your due, or that the master of the house will have it so. Contend not, lest you should trouble the company.

107. If others talk at table be attentive, but talk not with meat in your mouth.

108. When you speak of God or His attributes, let it be seriously and with reverence. Honor and obey your natural parents although they be poor.

109. Let your recreations be manful not sinful.

110. Labor to keep alive in your breast that little spark of celestial fire called conscience.

3

What Washington

Wrote And Spoke

On July 8, 1755, just after a bloody enemy encounter, Washington wrote to his brother, John A. Washington: *"But by the all-powerful dispensations of Providence, I have been protected beyond all human probability or expectation; for I had four bullets through my coat, and two horses shot under me, yet escaped unhurt, although death was leveling my companions on every side of me!"*

It was a time when the Colonial leaders were trying to decide whether or not to cut their ties with England.

Washington wrote this in his diary on June 1, 1774: *"Went to church and fasted all day."*

Washington gave this order on July 4, 1775, while in his headquarters at Cambridge: *"The General most earnestly requires and expects a due observance of those articles of war established for the government of the Army which forbid profane cursing, swearing and drunkenness.*

"And in like manner he requires and expects of all officers and soldiers not engaged in actual duty, a punctual attendance of Divine services, to implore the blessing of Heaven upon the  *means used for our safety and defense."*

43

On July 9, 1776, the Continental Congress authorized the providing of chaplains for Continental Army.

General Washington immediately gave the order to appoint a chaplain to every regiment of the Continental Army: *"The General hopes and trusts that every officer and man, will endeavor so to live, and act, as becomes a Christian Soldier defending the dearest Rights and Liberties of his country."*

This order was issued by Washington on July 20,1776: *"The General orders this day to be religiously observed by the forces under his Command, exactly in manner directed by the Continental Congress.*

"It is therefore strictly enjoined on all officers and soldiers to attend Divine service.

"And it is expected that all those who go to worship do take their arms, ammunition and accoutrements, and are prepared for immediate action, if called upon."

On May 2, 1778, General Washington was with his troops at Valley Forge.

He declared: *"While we are zealously performing the duties of good citizens and soldiers, we certainly ought not to be inattentive* to the higher duties of religion.

"To the distinguished character of Patriot, it should be our highest Glory to laud the more distinguished Character of Christian.

"The signal instances of Providential goodness which we have experienced and which have now almost crowned our labors with complete success demand from us in a peculiar manner the warmest returns of gratitude and piety to the Supreme Author of all good."

On August 20, 1778, General George Washington wrote a letter to Brigadier-General Thomas Nelson in Virginia.

He told his long time friend: *"The hand of Providence has been so conspicuous in all this (the course of the war) that he must be worse than an infidel that lacks faith, and more wicked that has not gratitude to acknowledge his obligations; but it will be time enough for me to turn Preacher when my present appointment ceases."*

British troops under Lord Cornwallis surrendered at Yorktown on October 19, 1781.

On October 20, Washington ordered a special church service to give thanks to God: *"The commander-in-chief earnestly recommends that the troops not on duty should universally attend with that seriousness of deportment and gratitude of heart which the recognition of such reiterated and astonishing interposition of Providence demands of us.*"

General Washington wrote to Thomas McKean, President of the Continental Congress,

on November 15, 1781: *"I take a particular pleasure in acknowledging that the interposing Hand of Heaven, in the various instances of our extensive Preparation for this Operation (Yorktown), has been most conspicuous and remarkable.*"

When the Revolutionary War finally ended, General Washington wrote a farewell letter to the 13 Governors of the newly freed states.

It was sent from his headquarters in Newburgh, New York, and dated June 14, 1783.

In it he stated: *"I now make it my earnest prayer that God would have you, and the State over which you preside, in his holy protection...that he would most graciously be pleased to dispose us all to do justice, to love, mercy, and to demean*

ourselves with that charity, humility, and pacific temper of mind, which were the characteristics of the Divine Author of our blessed religion, and without an humble imitation of whose example in these things, we can never hope to be a happy nation."

General Washington addressed Congress while at the Capitol of Maryland in Annapolis on December 23, 1783.

His speech was with regard to the official resignation of his military commission: *"I resign with satisfaction the appointment ... my abilities to accomplish so arduous a task, were superseded by ... the patronage of Heaven.*

"My gratitude for the interposition of Providence ... increases with every review of the momentous contest. ...

"I consider it an indispensable duty to close this last solemn act of my Official life by commending the Interest of our dearest Country to the protection of Almighty God, and those who have the superintendence of them, to His holy keeping."

"The pew I hold in the Episcopal Church at Alexandria, shall be charged with an annual rent of five pounds, Virginia money; and I promise to pay annually, to the minister and vestry of the Protestant Episcopal Church in Fairfax parish." (*April* 25th, 1785)

General Benjamin Lincoln was a deputy to General Washington during the War.

He was the officer who was instructed to accept the sword from General Cornwallis when the British surrendered at Yorktown.

Lincoln received a letter from General Washington dated June 29, 1788, that read: *"No Country upon Earth ever had it more in its power to attain these blessings. ...*

"Much to be regretted indeed would it be, were we to neglect the means and depart from the road which Providence has pointed us to, so plainly; I cannot believe it will ever come to pass.

"The Great Governor of the Universe has led us too long and too far ... to forsake us in the midst of it. ...

"We may, now and then, get bewildered; but I hope and trust that there is good sense and virtue enough left to recover the right path."

Jonathan Trumbull was the British Governor of Connecticut who changed sides and became a strong supporter of America's quest for independence.

Washington wrote this man on July 20, 1788, and said in part: *"We may, with a kind of grateful and pious exultation, trace the finger of Providence through those dark and mysterious events, which first induced the States to appoint a general Convention and then led them one after another into an adoption of the system recommended by that general Convention; thereby in all human probability, laying a lasting foundation for tranquility and happiness."*

George Washington was prepared to take the oath of office on April 30, 1789..

He stood with his hand on an open *Bible* while the on the balcony of Federal Hall, in New York City.

Embarrassed by the loudly pealing church bells, the booming cannon noise and the deafening ovation, he went inside to deliver his Inaugural Speech to both Houses of Congress.

The new President proclaimed in part: *"Such being the impressions under which I* have, in obedience to the public summons, repaired to the present station, it would be peculiarly improper to omit, in this first official act, my fervent supplications to that Almighty Being who rules over the universe, who presides in the councils of nations and whose providential aids can supply every human defect, that His benediction may consecrate to the liberties and happiness of the people of the United States a Government instituted by themselves for these essential purposes; and may enable every instrument employed in its administration to execute with success, the functions allotted to his charge.

"In tendering this homage to the Great Author of every public and private good, I assure myself that it expresses your sentiments not less than my own; nor those of my fellow-citizens at large, less than either.

"No people can be bound to acknowledge and adore the Invisible Hand which conducts the affairs of men more than the people of the United States.

"Every step by which they have advanced to the character of an independent nation seems to have been distinguished by some token of providential agency."

Washington once declared to an assembly of the Episcopal Church: "That

Government alone can be approved by Heaven, which promotes peace and secures protection to its Citizens in everything that is dear and interesting to them. ... "

The Quakers were holding their annual get-together at for Maryland, Delaware, New Jersey, Pennsylvania and the western part of Virginia in October of 1789.

President Washington addressed them in this manner: *"The liberty enjoyed by the People of these States of worshipping Almighty God agreeable to their consciences is not only among the choicest of their blessings, but also of their rights.*

"While men perform their social duties faithfully, they do all that society or the state can with propriety demand or expect; and remain responsible only to their Maker for the religion, or modes of faith, which they may prefer or profess."

A *National Day of Thanksgiving Proclamation* was issued by Washington on October 3, 1789, in which he said in part: *"Whereas it is the duty of all nations to acknowledge the providence of Almighty God, to obey His will, to be grateful for his benefits, and humbly to implore His protection and favor. ... Now therefore, I do recommend and assign Thursday, the twenty-sixth day of November next, to be devoted by the people of these United States. ... that we then may all unite unto him our sincere and humble thanks for His kind*  *care and protection of the people of this country previous to their becoming a nation; for the signal and manifold mercies and the favorable interpositions of His providence in the course and conclusion of the late war; ..."*

In a letter of March 11, 1792, President Washington wrote: *"I am sure that never was a people, who had more reason to acknowledge a Divine interposition in their affairs, than those of the United States; and I should be pained to believe that they have forgotten that agency, which was so often manifested during our Revolution, or that they failed to consider the omnipotence of that God who is alone able to protect them."*

In a letter to the congregation of the New Christian Church in Baltimore, Maryland, President George Washington exclaimed on January 27, 1793: *"We have abundant reason to rejoice that in this Land the light of truth and reason has triumphed over the power of bigotry and superstition, and that every person may here worship God according to the dictates of his own heart. In this enlightened Age and in this Land of equal liberty it is our boast, that a man's religious tenets will not forfeit the protection of the Laws, nor deprive him of the right of attaining and holding the highest offices that are known in the United States.*"

Another National Day of Thanksgiving Proclamation was issued by President Washington on January 1, 1795: *"It is in an especial manner our duty as a people, with devout reverence and affectionate gratitude, to acknowledge our many and great obligations to Almighty God, and to implore Him to continue and confirm the blessings we experienced. ...*

"Deeply penetrated with this sentiment, I, George Washington, President of the United States, do recommend to all religious societies and denominations, and to all persons whomsoever within the United States, to set apart and observe Thursday, the 19th day of February next, as a day of public thanksgiving and prayer."

4

Other Quotes

Of

Great Interest

"May the same wonder-working Deity, who long since delivering the Hebrews from their Egyptian Oppressors planted them in the promised land— whose providential agency has lately been conspicuous in establishing these United States as an independent Nation—still continue to water them with the dews of Heaven and to make the inhabitants of every denomination participate in the temporal and spiritual blessings of that people whose God is Jehovah."

"As the contempt of the religion of a country, by ridiculing any of its ceremonies, or affronting its Ministers ... , has ever been deeply resented, you are to be particularly careful, to restrain every officer and soldier from such imprudence and folly, and to punish every instance of it."

"The blessing and protection of Heaven are, at a times, necessary; but, especially so, in times of public distress and danger."

"Liberty, honor, and safety, are all at stake; and, trust, Providence will smile upon our efforts, and establish us, once more, the inhabitants of a free and happy country."

"In having pleased the Almighty Ruler of the Universe, to defend the cause of the United American States, and finally to raise us up a powerful friend among the Princes of the earth, to establish our

liberty and independency upon a lasting foundation."

"It will ever be the first wish of my heart, to inculcate a due sense of the dependence we ought to place in that All-Wise and. Powerful Being, on whom alone our success depends."

"In no instance, since the commencement of the war, has the interposition of Providence appeared more remarkably conspicuous, than in the rescue of the post and garrison of West Point from Arnold's villainous perfidy. I most devoutly congratulate my country, and every well-wisher to the cause, on this signal stroke of Providence."

"The Commander-in-chief earnestly recommends, that the troops not on duty should universally attend, with that seriousness of deportment and gratitude of heart, which the recognition of such reiterated and astonishing interpositions of Providence demands of US."

"We have abundant reasons to thank Providence, for its many favorable interpositions in our behalf. It has, at times, been my only dependence; for, all other resources seemed to have failed us."

"The Great Director of events has carried us through a variety of scenes, during this long and bloody contest, in which we have been, for seven campaigns, most nobly struggling."

"I commend my friends, and, with them, the interests and happiness of our dear country, to the keeping and protection of Almighty God."

"I earnestly pray, that the Omnipotent Being, who has not deserted the cause of America in the hour of its extreme hazard, may never yield so fair a heritage to anarchy or despotism."

"I commend my friends, and, with them, the interests and happiness of our dear country, to the keeping and protection of Almighty God."

"The vicissitudes of war are in the hands of the Supreme Director, where there is no control."

"The propitious smiles of Heaven can never be expected, on a nation that disregards the eternal rules of order and right, which Heaven itself has ordained."

"May we unite, in most humbly offering our prayers and supplications to the Great Lord and Ruler of Nations, and beseech him to pardon our national and other transgressions; ... to render our national government a blessing to all the people, by constantly being a government of wise, just, and constitutional laws, discreetly and faithfully executed and obeyed; to protect and guide. all sovereigns and nations, (especially such as have shown kindness to us), and to bless them with good governments ... as He alone knows to be best."

"I have often expressed my sentiments, that every man, conducting himself as a good citizen, and being accountable to God alone for his religious opinions, ought to be protected, in worshipping the Deity according to the dictates of his own conscience."

"I shall always strive, to prove faithful and impartial patron of genuine, vital religion." (1789)

"It is the duty of all nations, to acknowledge the Providence of Almighty God, to obey his will, to be grateful for his benefits, and humbly to implore his protection and favor."

"It would be peculiarly improper to omit, in this first official act, my fervent supplications to that Almighty Being who rules over the universe, who presides in the councils of nations ... that His benediction may consecrate, to the liberties and happiness of the people of the United States, a government instituted by themselves for these essential purposes ... ."

"No people can be bound to acknowledge and adore the invisible hand which conducts the affairs of men, more than the people of the United States."

"Providence has heretofore taken us up when all other means and hope seemed to be departing from us. In this I will confide."

"The Great Ruler of Events will not permit the happiness of so many millions to be destroyed."

"I humbly implore that Being, on who's Will the fate of nations depends, to crown with success our endeavors ... ."

"Let us unite, in imploring the Supreme Ruler of Nations, to spread his holy protection over these United States; to turn the machinations of the wicked, to the confirming of our Constitution; to enable us, at all times, to root out internal sedition, and put invasion to flight; to perpetuate to our country that prosperity, which His goodness has already conferred, and to verify the anticipations of this government being a safeguard of human rights."

"It is impossible to govern the universe, without the aid of a Supreme Being."

"It is impossible to account for the creation of the universe, without the agency of a Supreme Being."

5

Prayers

Of

Washington

While a General

And As Our

President

The following prayers are those found in George Washington's personal field notebook. There were a total of 24 pages, each of which was written by this great man. They certainly reveal the depth of his character.

1

Sunday Morning

Almighty God, and most merciful Father, who didst command the children of Israel to offer a daily sacrifice to thee, that thereby they might glorify and praise thee for thy protection both night and day, receive, O Lord, my morning sacrifice which I now offer up to thee; I yield thee humble and hearty thanks that thou has preserved me from the danger of the night past, and brought me to the light of the day, and the comforts thereof, a day which is consecrated to Thine own service and for thine own honor. Let my heart, therefore, Gracious God, be so affected with the glory and majesty of it, that I may not do mine own works, but wait on thee, and discharge those weighty duties thou requirest of me, and since thou art a God of pure eyes, and wilt be sanctified in all who draw near unto thee, who doest not regard the sacrifice of fools, nor hear sinners who tread in thy courts, pardon, I beseech thee, my sins, remove them from thy presence, as far as the east is from the west, and accept of me for the merits of thy son Jesus Christ, that when I come into thy temple, and compass thine altar, my prayers may come before thee as incense; and as thou wouldst hear me calling upon thee in my prayers, so give me grace to hear thee calling on me in thy word, that it may be wisdom, righteousness, reconciliation and peace to the saving of the soul in the day of the Lord Jesus. Grant that I may hear it with reverence, receive it with meekness, mingle it with faith, and that it may accomplish in me, Gracious God, the good work for which thou has sent it. Bless my family, kindred, friends and country, be our God & guide this day and for ever for his sake, who ay down in the Grave and arose again for us, Jesus Christ our Lord, Amen.

2

Sunday Evening

O most Glorious God, in Jesus Christ my merciful and loving father, I acknowledge and confess my guilt, in the weak and imperfect performance of the duties of this day. I have called on thee for pardon and forgiveness of sins, but so coldly and carelessly, that my prayers are become my sin and stand in need of pardon. I have heard thy holy word, but with such deadness of spirit that I have been an unprofitable and forgetful hearer, so that, O Lord, tho' I have done thy work, yet it hath been so negligently that I may rather expect a curse than a blessing from thee. But, O God, who art rich in mercy and plenteous in redemption, mark not, I beseech thee, what I have done amiss; remember that I am but dust, and remit my transgressions, negligences & ignorances, and cover them all with the absolute obedience of thy dear Son, that those sacrifices which I have offered may be accepted by thee, in and for the sacrifice of Jesus Christ offered upon the cross for me; for his sake, ease me of the burden of my sins, and give me grace that by the call of the Gospel I may rise from the slumber of sin into the newness of life. Let me live according to those holy rules which thou hast this day prescribed in thy holy word; make me to know what is acceptable in thy holy word; make me to know what is acceptable in thy sight, and therein to delight, open the eyes of my understanding, and help me thoroughly to examine myself concerning my knowledge, faith and repentance, increase my faith, and direct me to the true object Jesus Christ the way, the truth and the life, bless O Lord, all the people of this land, from the highest to the lowest, particularly those whom thou has appointed to rule over us in church & state. continue thy goodness to me this night. These weak petitions I humbly implore thee to hear accept and ans. for the sake of thy Dear Son Jesus Christ our Lord, Amen.

3

Monday Morning

O eternal and everlasting God, I presume to present myself this morning before thy Divine majesty, beseeching thee to accept of my humble and hearty thanks, that it hath pleased thy great goodness to keep and preserve me the night past from all the dangers poor mortals are subject to, and has given me sweet and pleasant sleep, whereby I find my body refreshed and comforted for performing the duties of this day, in which I beseech thee to defend me from all perils of body and soul. Direct my thoughts, words and work, wash away my sins in the immaculate blood of the lamb, and purge my heart by thy holy spirit, from the dross of my natural corruption, that I may with more freedom of mind and liberty of will serve thee, the ever lasting God, in righteousness and holiness this day, and all the days of my life. Increase my faith in the sweet promises of the gospel; give me repentance from dead works; pardon my wanderings, & direct my thoughts unto thyself, the God of my salvation; teach me how to live in thy fear, labor in thy service, and ever to run in the ways of thy commandments; make me always watchful over my heart, that neither the terrors of conscience, the loathing of holy duties, the love of sin, nor an unwillingness to depart this life, may cast me into a spiritual slumber, but daily frame me more

7 more into the likeness of thy son Jesus Christ, that living in thy fear, and dying in thy favor, I may in thy appointed time attain the resurrection of the just unto eternal life bless my family, friends & kindred unite us all in praising & glorifying thee in all our works begun, continued, and ended, when we shall come to make our last account before thee blessed savior, who hath taught us thus to pray, our Father, & c.

4

Monday Evening

Most Gracious Lord God, from whom proceedeth every good and perfect gift, I offer to thy divine majesty my unfeigned praise & thanksgiving for all thy mercies towards me. Thou mad'st me at first and hast ever since sustained the work of thy own hand; thou gav'st thy Son to die for me; and hast given me assurance of salvation, upon my repentance and sincerely endeavoring to conform my life to his holy precepts and example. Thou art pleased to lengthen out to me the time of repentance and to move me to it by thy spirit and by the word, by thy mercies, and by thy judgments; out of a deepness of thy mercies, and by my own unworthiness, I do appear before thee at this time; I have sinned and done very wickedly, be merciful to me, O God, and pardon me for Jesus Christ sake; instruct me in the particulars of my duty, and suffer me not to be tempted above what thou givest me strength to bear. Take care, I pray thee of my affairs and more and more direct me in thy truth, defend me from my enemies, especially my spiritual ones. Suffer me not to be drawn from thee, by the blandishments of the world, carnal desires, the cunning of the devil, or deceitfulness of sin. work in me thy good will and pleasure, and discharge my mind from all things that are displeasing to thee, of all ill will and discontent, wrath and bitterness, pride & vain conceit of myself, and render me charitable, pure, holy, patient and heavenly minded. be with me at the hour of death; dispose me for it, and deliver me from the slavish fear of it, and make me willing and fit to die whenever thou shalt call me hence. Bless our rulers in church and state. bless O Lord the whole race of mankind, and let the world be filled with the knowledge of Thee and thy son Jesus Christ. Pity the sick, the poor, the weak, the needy, the widows and fatherless, and all that morn or are broken in heart, and be merciful to them according to their several necessities. bless my friends and grant me grace to forgive my enemies as heartily as I desire forgiveness of Thee my heavenly Father. I beseech thee to defend me this night from all evil, and do more for me than I can think or ask, for Jesus Christ sake, in whose most

holy name & words, I continue to pray, Our Father,
& c.

5

Tuesday Morning

O Lord our God, most mighty and merciful
father, I thine unworthy creature and servant, do once
more approach thy presence. Though not worthy to
appear before thee, because of my natural
corruptions, and the many sins and transgressions
which I have committed against thy divine majesty;
yet I beseech thee, for the sake of him in whom thou
art well pleased, the Lord Jesus Christ, to admit me
to render thee deserved thanks and praises for thy
manifold mercies extended toward me, for the quiet
rest & repose of the past night, for food, rainment,
health, peace, liberty, and the hopes of a better life
through the merits of thy dear son's bitter passion.
and O kind father continue thy mercy and favor to
me this day, and ever hereafter; propose all my
lawful undertakings; et me have all my directions
from thy holy spirit; and success from thy bountiful
hand. Let the bright beams of thy light so shine into
my heart, and enlighten my mind in understanding
thy blessed word, that I may be enabled to perform
thy will in all things, and effectually resist all

temptations of the world, the flesh and the devil. preserve and defend our rulers in church & state. bless the people of this land, be a father to the fatherless, a comforter to the comfortless, a deliverer to the captives, and a physician to the sick. Let thy blessings guide this day and forever through J. C. in whose blessed form of prayer I conclude my weak petitions--Our Father, & c.

6

Tuesday Evening

Most gracious God and heavenly father, we cannot cease, but must cry unto thee for mercy, because my sins cry against me for justice. How shall I address myself unto thee, I must with the publican stand and admire at thy great goodness, tender mercy, and long suffering towards me, in that thou hast kept me the past day from being consumed and brought to naught. O Lord, what is man, or the son of man, that thou regardest him; the more days pass over my head, the more sins and iniquities I heap up against thee. If I should cast up the account of my good deeds done this day, how few and small would they be; but if I should reckon my miscarriages, surely they would be many and great. O, blessed father, let thy son's blood wash me from all impurities, and cleanse me from the stains of sin that are upon me. Give me grace to lay hold upon his merits; that they may be my reconciliation and atonement unto thee,--That I may know my sins are forgiven by his death & passion. embrace me in the arms of thy mercy; vouchsafe to receive me unto the bosom of thy love, shadow me with thy wings, that I may safely rest under thy suspicion this night; and so into thy hands I commend myself, both soul and body, in the name of thy son, J. C., beseeching Thee, when this life shall end, I may take my everlasting rest with thee in thy heavenly kingdom. bless all in authority over us, be merciful to all those afflicted with thy cross or calamity, bless all my friends, forgive my enemies and accept my thanksgiving this evening for all the mercies and favors afforded me; hear and graciously answer these my requests, and whatever else thou see'st needful grant us, for the sake of Jesus Christ in whose blessed name and words I continue to pray, Our Father, & c.

7

Wednesday Morning

Almighty and eternal Lord God, the great creator of heaven & earth, and the God and Father of our Lord Jesus Christ; look down from heaven, in pity and compassion upon me thy servant, who humbly prostrate myself before thee, sensible of thy mercy and my own misery; there is an infinite distance between thy glorious majesty and me, thy poor creature, the work of thy hand, between thy infinite power, and my weakness, thy wisdom, and my folly, thy eternal Being, and my mortal frame, but, O Lord, I have set myself at a greater distance from thee by my sin and wickedness, and humbly acknowledge the corruption of my nature and the many rebellions of my life. I have sinned against heaven and before thee, in thought, word & deed; I have contemned thy majesty and holy laws. I have likewise sinned by omitting what I ought to do, and committing what I ought not. I have rebelled against light, despised thy mercies and judgments, and broken my vows and promises; I have neglected the means of Grace, and opportunities of becoming better; my iniquities are multiplies, and my sins are very great. I confess them, O Lord, with shame and sorrow, detestation and loathing, and desire to be vile in my own eyes, as I have rendered myself vile in thine. I humbly beseech thee to be merciful to me in the free pardon of my sins, for the sake of thy dear Son, my only savior, J. C., who came not to call the righteous, but sinners to repentance; be pleased to renew my nature and write thy laws upon my heart, and help me to live, righteously, soberly, and godly in this evil worlds; make me humble, meek, patient and contented, and work in me the grace of thy holy spirit. Prepare me for death and judgment, and let the thoughts thereof awaken me to a greater care and study to approve myself unto thee in well doing. bless our rulers in church & state. Help all in affliction or adversity--give them patience and a sanctified use of their affliction, and in thy good time deliverance from them; forgive my enemies, take me unto thy protection this day, keep me in perfect peace, which I ask in the name & for the sake of Jesus. Amen.

8

Wednesday Evening

Holy and eternal Lord God who art the King of heaven, and the watchman of Israel, that never slumberest or sleepest, what shall we render unto thee for all thy benefits; because thou hast inclined thine ears unto me, therefore will I call on thee as long as I live, from the rising of the sun to the going down of the same let thy name be praised. among the infinite riches of thy mercy towards me, I desire to render thanks & praise for thy merciful preservation of me this day, as well as all the days of my life; and for the many other blessings & mercies spiritual & temporal which thou hast bestowed on me, contrary to my deserving. All these thy mercies call on me to be thankful and my infirmities & wants call for a continuance of thy tender mercies; cleanse my soul, O Lord, I beseech thee, from whatever is offensive to thee, and hurtful to me, and give me what is convenient for me. watch over me this night, and give me comfortable and sweet sleep to fit me for the service of the day following. Let my soul watch for the coming of the Lord Jesus; let my bed put me in mind of my grave, and my rising from there of my last resurrection; O heavenly Father, so frame this heart of mine, that I may ever delight to live according to thy will and command, in holiness and righteousness before thee all the days of my life. Let me remember, O Lord, the time will come when the trumpet shall sound, and the dead shall rise and stand before the judgment seat, and give an account of whatever they have done in the body, and let me so prepare my soul, that I may do it with joy and not with grief. bless the rulers and people of this and forget not those who are under any affliction or oppression. Let thy favor be extended to all my relations friends and all others who I ought to remember in my prayer and hear me I beseech thee for the sake of my dear redeemer in whose most holy words, I farther pray, Our Father, & c.

9

Thursday Morning

Most gracious Lord God, whose dwelling is in the highest heavens, and yet beholdest the lowly and humble upon the earth, I blush and am ashamed to lift up my eyes to thy dwelling place, because I have sinned against thee; look down, I beseech thee upon me thy unworthy servant who prostrate myself at the footstool of thy mercy, confessing my own guiltiness, and begging pardon for my sins; what couldst thou have done Lord more for me, or what could I have done more against thee? Thou didst send me thy Son to take nature upon.

NOTE: The prayer book ended on this page. Were the rest of Washington's prayer pages lost? Or did he not complete his prayer list? This has never been determined.

Other Prayers of Washington

Washington's Prayer on May 1, 1777, when he received the news that France was joining the Colonies in the War for American Independence:

"And now, Almighty Father, if it is Thy holy will that we shall obtain a place and name among the nations of the earth, grant that we may be enabled to show our gratitude for Thy goodness by our endeavors to fear and obey Thee. Bless us with Thy wisdom in our counsels, success in battle, and let all our victories be tempered with humanity. Endow, also, our enemies with enlightened minds, that they become sensible of their injustice, and willing to restore our liberty and peace. Grant the petition of Thy servant, for the sake of Him whom Thou hast called Thy beloved Son; nevertheless, not my will, but Thine be done."

Washington's Prayer On a Plaque

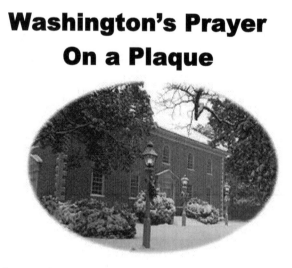

Washington's Prayer has been preserved for

posterity on the plaque at Pohick Church in Fairfax, Virginia. Washington was a vestryman there from 1762 to 1784. It is also to be found on a plaque in New York City's St. Paul's Chapel:

"Almighty God; We make our earnest prayer that Thou wilt keep the United States in Thy Holy protection; and Thou wilt incline the hearts of the Citizens to cultivate a spirit of subordination and obedience to Government; and entertain a brotherly affection and love for one(another and for their fellow Citizens of the United States at large, and particularly for their brethren who have served in the Field.

"And finally that Thou wilt most graciously be pleased to dispose us all to do justice, to love mercy, and to demean ourselves with that Charity, humility, and pacific temper of mind which were the Characteristics of the Divine Author of our blessed Religion, and without a humble imitation of whose example in these things we can never hope to be a happy nation.

"Grant our supplication, we beseech Thee, through Jesus Christ our Lord. Amen."

Other Titles
By
This Author

HISTORICAL COOK BOOKS
Cooking & Baking Recipes
From the
War of Northern Aggression
8" x 10" 276 pages $17.95
Order From: createspace.com/3420014

Historical Thanksgiving Cooking
And Baking
5.5 x 8.5   257 pages $14.95
Order From: createspace.com/3578977

Historical Christmas Cooking
In America
5.5 x 8.5   275 pages $14.95
Order From: createspace.com/3486039

A Treasury of Civil War Family Recipes
5.5 x 8.5   235 pages $14.95
Order From: createspace.com/3477320

A Treasury of Family Recipes
From the Time of the War
For American Independence
5.5 x 8.5   255 pages $14.95
Order From: createspace.com/3551835

**Baking Recipes and Home Remedies
From The Time of the War
For American Independence**
5.5 x 8.5   235 pages $14.95
Order From: createspace.com/3480754

POLITICAL DYNAMITE
**Unwanted Dead or Alive
The Betrayal of American POWs
Following
World War II, Korea and Vietnam**
5.5" x 8.5" 487 pages $24.95
Order From: createspace.com/3565025

**Unwanted Dead or Alive
The Betrayal of American POWs
Following
World War II, Korea and Vietnam**
8" x 10" 409 pages $24.95
Order From: createspace.com/3426306

**Unwanted Dead or Alive
The Betrayal of American POWs
Following
World War II, Korea and Vietnam**

Part 1
8" x 10" 170 pages $12.00
Order From: ceatespace.com/3461216

Unwanted Dead or Alive
The Betrayal of American POWs
Following
World War II, Korea and Vietnam
Part 2
8" x 10" 186 pages $12.00
Order From: createspace.com/3461245

Unwanted Dead or Alive
The Betrayal of American POWs
Following
World War II, Korea and Vietnam
Part 3
8" x 10" 132 pages $12.00
Order From: createspace.com/3461267

The McCarthy Chronicles
Part 1
Treason
5.5" x 8.5" 445 pages $24.95
Order From: createspace.com/3471179

The McCarthy Chronicles
Part 2
Traitors
5.5" x 8.5" 501 pages $24.95
Order From: createspace.com/3470924

AMERICAN HISTORY BOOKS
Historic Days in 1776
The Declaration of Independence
5.5" x 8.5" 276 pages $14.95
Order From: createspace.com/9426527

The Prophetic Vision
Of General George Washington
at Valley Forge
5.5" x8.5" 171 pages $14.95
Order From: createspace.com/3427309

George Washington's
Prophetic Dream at Valley Forge
5.5" x 8.5" 106 pages $9.95
Order From: createspace.com/3430107

George Washington's Prayers

5.5" x 8.5" 88 pages $9.95
Order From: createspace.com/3569091

George Washington – Chosen By God
5.5" x 8.5" 289 pages $14.95
Order From: createspace.com/3653951

George Washington – Man of Destiny
5.5" x 8.5" 301 pages $14.95
Order From: createspace.com/3491125

Men of Destiny
5.5" x 8.5" 289 pages $14.95
Order From: createspace.com/3693853

HOW TO OR SELF HELP
The Write Stuff
The Perfect Handbook
For Achieving Writing Success
5.5" x 8.5" 452 pages $24.95
Order From: createspace.com/3431896

Orders For Resale
40% Off Retail Price

Send Purchase Order To:
Christianamerica2@yahoo.com

Made in the USA
Middletown, DE
12 May 2019